BLUES LICKS FOR PIANO

BY BLAKE NEELY

Cover artwork by Levin Pfeufer

Cherry Lane Music Company
Director of Publications/Project Editor: Mark Phillips

ISBN 978-1-57560-165-6

Visit our website at www.cherrylaneprint.com

CONTENTS

INTRODUCTION

First of all, welcome. Secondly, thanks for choosing this book.

I hope it will be a fun way to learn more about making great-sounding blues music on your piano or keyboard. Along the way, you just might wind up being a better all-around piano player. Why? The techniques in blues piano employ skills that go beyond the type of music you're playing. Playing blues piano helps build finger dexterity, improvisational skills, and a better understanding of harmonic structure.

Maybe you already know about blues form: its rhythm, scales, and effects. That's fine, too. You'll still benefit from the many great blues licks and helpful hints that are packed inside the music in this book.

So, power on your electric keyboard or dust off your baby grand, and let's start singing the blues.

Have a good time.

ABOUT THE AUTHOR

Blake Neely is the best-selling author of many instructional music books, including *Piano for Dummies, FastTrack Music Instruction, How to Play from a Fake Book,* and *Pocket Guide Music Theory.* He is also an award-winning composer, arranger, orchestrator, and pianist.

Currently living in bluesy Austin, Texas, he continues to work on his own piano playing and hopefully create some new riffs and licks for you in future books.

W AT YOU S OULD KNOW

Before you start working your way through these pages, make sure you have a basic understanding of the following music fundamentals:

1. Basic piano-playing skills
2. Reading music from a treble clef and bass clef staff
3. Reading chord symbols
4. Reading rhythmic notation from whole notes to triplets
5. Counting to 12

If not, this book could be frustrating for you, since I intend to use super big, complex, meaty musical terms like *staff, clef, scale,* and others. (If you can't count to 12, well…*life* could be frustrating to you.)

SUGGESTED LISTENING

One of the very best ways to learn any kind of music is by listening to recordings. Hearing how the masters play gives you inspiration as well as ideas.

If you hear something you like, hurry over to your piano and try to replicate the sound or seek out published transcriptions. Here's a small sampling of some killer blues performers and their recordings:

Ray Charles, *Genius and Soul* (Rhino)

Duke Ellington, *Blues in Orbit* (Columbia)

Buddy Guy, *Very Best of Buddy Guy* (Rhino)

Dr. John, *Anthology* (Rhino)

Jerry Lee Lewis, *Rocket 88* (Rhino)

Professor Longhair, *Fess: Professor Longhair Anthology* (Rhino)

Little Richard, *The Specialty Sessions* (Specialty)

Memphis Slim, *Bluebird Sessions (1940–1941)* (RCA)

Jimmy Smith, *Back at the Chicken Shack* (Blue Note)

Roosevelt Sykes, *Roosevelt Sykes (1929–1941)* (Story of Blues)

W AT ARE T E BLUES?

For those of you who bought this book for its cool cover, without even knowing what the blues are, here's a brief explanation. (For those of you who already know, you might learn something new.)

BRIEF HISTORY OF THE BLUES

When most people think of the blues, they think of guitarists such as Eric Clapton, B.B. King, Stevie Ray Vaughan, Muddy Waters, and Robert Johnson. But the ol' 88 keys also has an important part in the blues music history.

Blues piano dates back to the very early years of the 20th century, in many cases predating jazz, stride, and ragtime styles.

With its easy chords, cool riffs, laid-back rhythm, and repetitive form, the blues fast became one of America's most popular music forms.

LEGENDARY PERFORMERS

The century has welcomed many legends to the Blues Piano Hall of Fame (a fictional place; I made it up). Do any of these names ring a bell?

Mose Allison, Albert Ammons, Marcia Ball, Count Basie, James Booker, Ray Bryant, Charles Brown (no, not Charlie), Henry Butler, Ray Charles, Cow-Cow Davenport, Detroit Junior, Fats Domino, Champion Jack Dupree, Duke Ellington, Buddy Guy, Dr. John, Dink Johnson, James P. Johnson, Jerry Lee Lewis, Ramsey Lewis, Professor Longhair, Junior Mance, Les McCann, Jimmy McGriff, Little Brother Montgomery, Alex Moore, "Jelly Roll" Morton, Pinetop Perkins, Billy Preston, Piano Red, Little Richard, Memphis Slim, Sunnyland Slim ("Slim" is a pretty popular blues name), Jimmy Smith, Otis Spann, Roosevelt Sykes, Fats Waller, Mary Lou Williams, Steve Winwood, Stevie Wonder, and Jimmy Yancey.

Each has his own remarkable style, and each comes from a very different time in blues history, but each of them is a legend.

Maybe you'll be on this list one day!

FORM AND RHYTHM

Two musical elements that help distinguish the blues from other music styles are its *form* and its *rhythm*. As you read on, you'll learn more about each of these elements, but here are some very basic differences to tide you over:

The *form* is usually several 12-bar or 8-bar musical phrases, repeated again and again with changes in the lyrics or instrumentation. The harmonic progression, however, stays the same over each 12-bar or 8-bar phrase.

The *rhythm* is generally laid-back, a swing-type rhythm which sounds like long-short, long-short triplets.

More on these elements in the pages to follow...I promise!

Lyrics to Make You Cry

If you don't recognize the music as blues by its performer, rhythm, form, or overall sound, the lyrics are usually a dead giveaway.

Often the lyrics to a blues tune will be about somebody losing something or someone. Perhaps they were wronged in some way, or maybe they just feel downright bad. (With the occasional exception, they usually aren't singing about winning the lottery.)

Here are two sample lyrics for a blues song:

I woke up this morning, my dog was gone
Yeah, I woke up this morning, and my dog was gone
I don't know why he left me, and I just bought him a new bone

My baby was crying all night and all day
I said my baby was crying all night and all day
Asked her why she cried and she said, "Cause you won't go away"

Why all the sadness? Um, it is called the "blues," you know, not the "happies."

CHORDING THE BLUES

Like any musical style, you'll encounter tons and tons of different chords and harmonies in blues music. Anything from simple major triads to complex "♭9," "add 11," and other amalgamated chords.

There are, of course, a handful of chords that are used over and over again in blues music. Here are some examples.

COMMON CHORDS

The three most common types of chords in the blues are major, minor, and seventh (not necessarily in that order). And specifically the *tonic, subdominant,* and *dominant* chords. (That is, the chords formed on the first, fourth, and fifth scale degrees.)

You don't have to know much about music theory (or piano playing, for that matter) to know these three chord types. But just to make sure I don't lose you as early as page 6, here's a really brief chord primer:

Major chords contain the root note, major 3rd, and perfect 5th intervals.

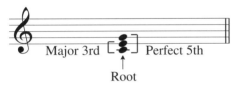

Minor chords contain the root note, minor 3rd, and perfect 5th intervals.

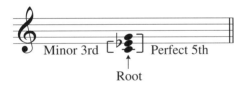

Seventh chords add the minor 7th interval to a major or minor chord.

ROMAN NUMERAL CHORD NAMING

Quite frequently, chords in blues music are named by a Roman numeral, which refers to the scale degree used as the chord's root. This way, without a care in the world for what key you're playing in, the sad singer can tell the equally sad bandmates what the sad chord progression will be.

For example, if you have a chord progression of I–IV–I–V, in the key of C you would play C–F–C–G.

While in the key of G you would play the same I–IV–I–V progression as G–C–G–D.

Get used to referring to chords in this manner, and you'll be able to follow any blues singer or band. (If you have no intention of playing with others or ever transposing, then at least you'll know how to count when in Rome.)

A WORD ABOUT INVERSIONS

Don't be afraid to use chord inversions in the right hand. To *invert* a chord is to change the relative position of its notes; for example, a C chord played (bottom to top) C-E-G, can be inverted by playing (bottom to top) E-G-C or G-C-E. In most cases, using inversions provides the smoothest-sounding chord changes. Using inversions, notice how easy it is to change between the frequently used I, IV, and V chords.

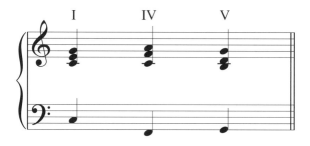

12-BAR FORM

I promised you a more detailed explanation of form, so here we go…

The most common form used in blues music is known as the *12-bar form*, but this doesn't mean that the song is only 12 bars long. (Heck, that could be about a 30-second song.)

No, it's called 12-bar because the entire chord progression is completed every 12 bars and then repeats. A blues song usually plays through the 12-bar progression at least four times.

Using major chords as an example, a 12-bar form might go like this:

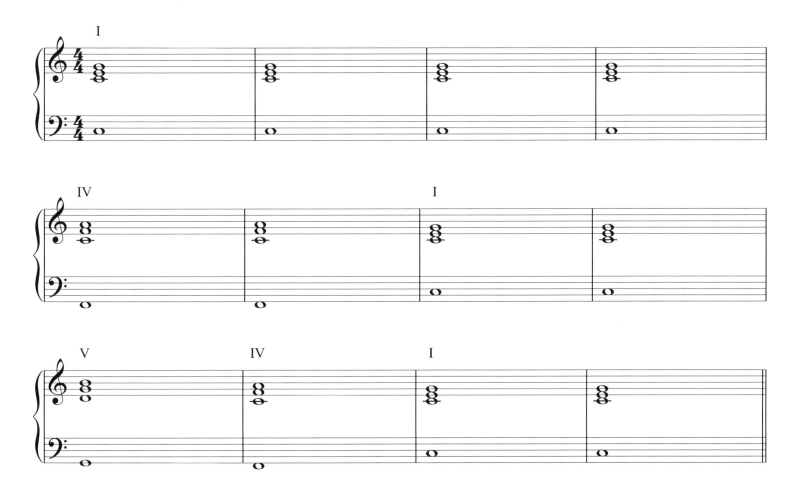

In fact, that's the basic chord progression in all 12-bar blues. Look at it again and notice the Roman numeral chords. The progression goes like this:

Chord	Number of Bars
I	4
IV	2
I	2
V	1
IV	1
I	2

Play this chord progression over and over while singing about how much you owe on your taxes this year, and you're certifiably playing the blues.

MINOR ADJUSTMENTS

Play the exact same chord progression again, but this time make all of the chords minor. (That is, lower the 3rd of each chord a half step.)

The minor chords help give the music a bit more of a sad sound. Now you can sing about your car breaking down, or something pathetic like that. With the right emotion, you're sure to get a ride from a sympathetic listener.

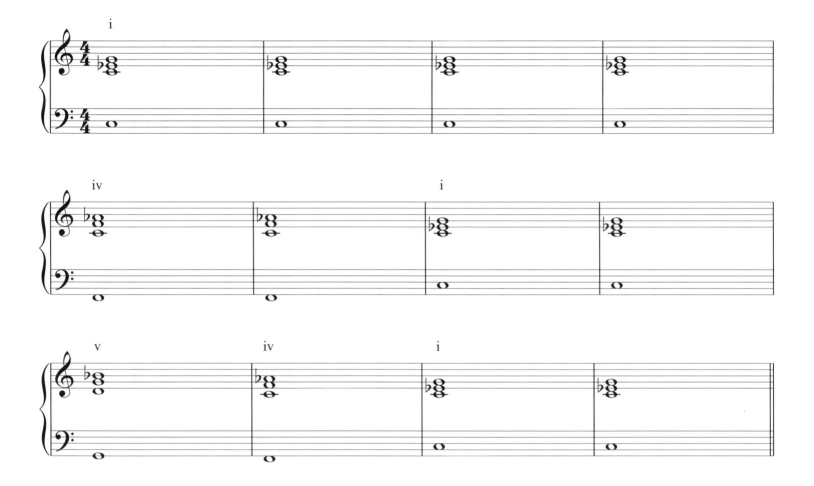

UNRESOLVED SEVENTHS

You probably know from all those music theory classes (or just from futzing around on the piano) that seventh chords provide musical tension, or *dissonance*.

And hey, when you have the blues, don't you feel the tension? That's why seventh chords are perfect for blues music.

Try the same chord progression as before (major or minor), but this time, add a minor seventh note to the chords. Notice that since the left hand is playing the root of the chord, the right hand can just play the 3rd, 5th, and 7th to preserve the lighter "sound" of a three-note rather than a four-note chord.

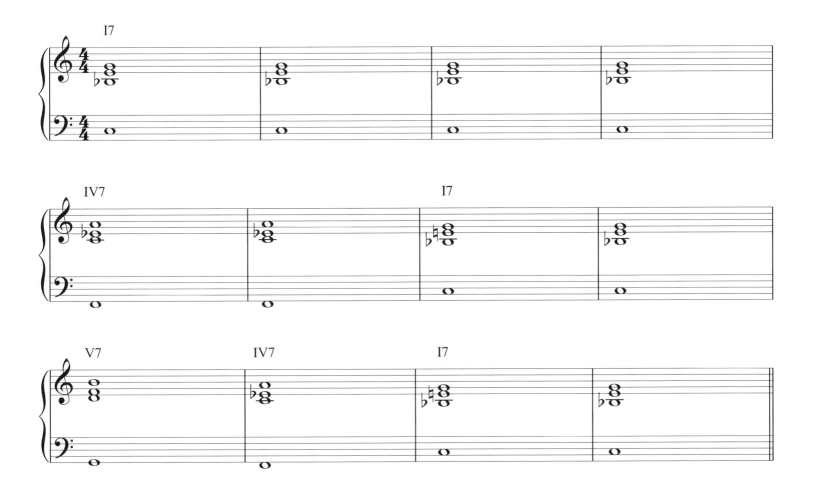

LITTLE SURPRISES

There are lots of ways to freshen up the potentially boring 12-bar chord progression. If you're playing with a band, a guitar or piano solo works well. But you can also keep the audience happy with a few simple chord substitutions thrown in.

Turnaround

This little chord surprise happens at the end of each 12-bar progression. It's called a *turnaround*, because it "turns" the form "around" to the beginning again. (Perhaps this isn't the real definition, but I like it!)

It's easy: just play a V7 chord in the last bar. This works whether you're playing major or minor chords. Just remember to play this last turnaround chord as a dominant seventh (not a minor seventh).

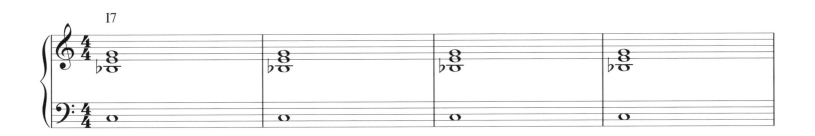

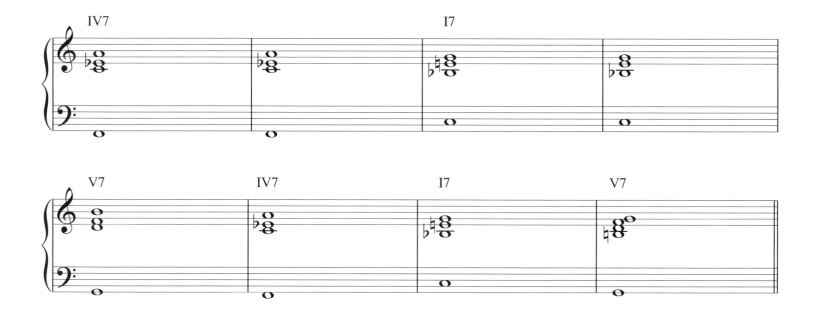

Quick Change

Next we can change a chord at the front of the phrase. In bar 2, change the I chord to a IV chord. Make sure it's the same type as the other chords (major or minor).

This is called a *quick change*, because you "quickly change" from the I to IV and back to I. And that's all there is to it. The rest of the phrase can stay as is, with or without a turnaround V7 at the end.

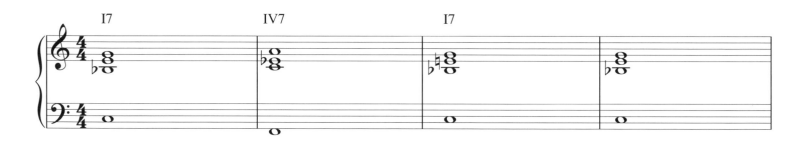

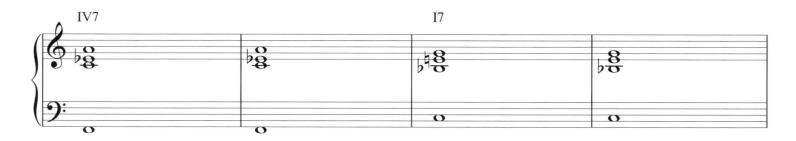

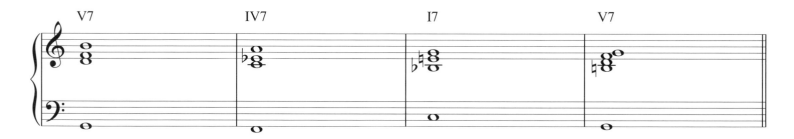

RHYTHM BREAK

As I said in the beginning, rhythm is a highly integral part of blues music. In fact, if you only heard the drum part of a song, you'd still probably know whether or not it's the blues because of its characteristic rhythmic feel.

In particular, two types of rhythmic figures are prominent in blues: *shuffle feel* and the *hambone*, or *Charleston*.

SHUFFLE FEEL

The simplest explanation of the shuffle or swing rhythm is that it sounds "long-short, long-short." What does that mean exactly?

Play through the next example of triplets and notice the "long-short" sound. The quarter note is, of course, slightly longer than the eighth note. By grouping them as a triplet, you get a more "laid-back, swingin'" feel.

Triplets aren't that tough to play. But what is tricky is the fact that you rarely see triplets notated in blues music. "What?" you ask. I'll explain…

The music is most often notated as "straight eighth notes" but with a little marking on the first bar, telling you to play any two eighth notes as a quarter-eighth triplet (shuffle):

Note: Sometimes you won't see that cool little marking. Instead, it will just say "Shuffle" or "Swing," which means…well, I'm sure you understand by now.

HAMBONES FROM CHARLESTON

The other important rhythm to have under your fingers carries with it perhaps my favorite musical term: *hambone*.

When playing just chords, try playing the hambone with your right hand, while your left hand pounds out steady quarter-note chords. The syncopated sound will create a terrific groove for the song.

Of course, you can also play the hambone with your left hand as an accompaniment to your right-hand solos. This takes a bit more practice but sounds great when you know what to do.

ANTICIPATION

Last, but not least, allow me to tell you about a little rhythmic trick that keeps the audience listening (and who does-n't want that?): *anticipation*.

This little effect derives its name from the fact that you are *anticipating* the beat. You did this once already with the hambone. You anticipated beat 3:

But take it a bit further and anticipate other strong beats (1 and 3) or weak beats (2 and 4) simply by playing the chord one eighth note early, like this:

Anticipating beats 1 and 3…

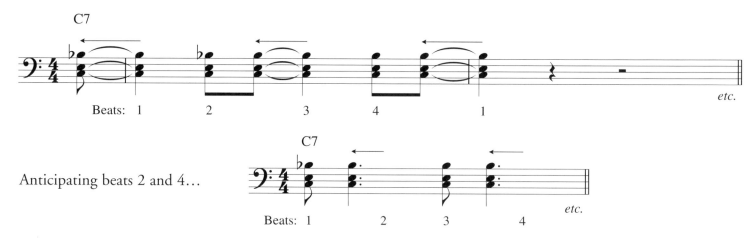

Anticipating beats 2 and 4…

Remember this rhythmic effect for left-hand chord accompaniments, solo riffs, or anything you play.

LEFT-HAND LICKS AND RIFFS

OK, get your hand out of your mouth. I'm talking about musical licks…

Playing chords is great, and you can play chords alone for days and still be playing the blues. But this can also start to sound a little stale after a while. A great way to make your chordal music more interesting is with some cool bass patterns.

Cool Bass Patterns

Here are a few ideas to get you started (not to mention keeping your left hand from getting bored).

Broken Chords

An easy solution is the ever-popular *arpeggio*, or "broken chord." For each right-hand chord, your left hand plays select notes from that chord.

It can be a three note pattern, consisting of the root, 3rd, and 5th…

It can be the root, 5th, and octave…

Or go all out with some dazzling seventh arpeggios…

Boogie Woogie All Night Long

You can liven things up with a *boogie-woogie* left-hand pattern, the likes of which can be heard in music by such legendary pianists as Jerry Lee Lewis, Dr. John, Little Richard, and many others.

All you do is move between a perfect 5th and a major 6th interval. For best results, use fingers 2 and 1 for these little changes.

This pattern works best underneath major or seventh chords, rather than minor chords.

Here Comes the Train

I don't know why, but this next pattern just sounds like a train locomotive. (Ever watch *Mister Rogers' Neighborhood*? Remember the sound of the Trolley coming to see him? Who knew it was a blues bass pattern?)

This one uses a perfect 5th interval followed by a ♭III and ♮III.

RHYTHMIC CHORDS

Or you can just play chords with your left hand, too. In fact, learning to do this is highly advisable. It leaves your right hand free to play cool solo riffs and licks. (And that's why you bought this book, right?)

Play straight quarter-note or eighth-note chords…

Play a hambone…

Or play a combination of both…

etc.

HELPING OUT THE CHORDS

Now combine both hands in a nice 12-bar chord progression, using all of the bass pattern options I gave you.

I'll give you the full progression with the boogie-woogie bass pattern for starters. Then, for the sake of saving valuable pages, the other patterns will be shown only as 4-bar examples. (Please feel free to keep them going for the entire 12-bar phrase…and about a hundred repeats.)

Boogie-Woogie

Broken Chords

Hambone

"Train"

Rhythmic Chords

THE SCALE TO END ALL SCALES

In addition to form, rhythm, and lyrics, another MVP in blues music is the scale used to create blues riffs and melodies. So closely related to the blues style is this scale that it's even called the *blues scale*.

Here it is, based on the root note C:

Step pattern = 1 1/2 –Whole–Half–Half–1 1/2–Whole

COMPARING TO MAJOR/MINOR

Compare that C blues scale side-by-side with the C major scale, and you'll quickly (hopefully) notice some key differences:

Compare it to a C natural minor scale, and you also find differences:

Indeed, this blues scale is a very unusual scale. Why?

1. Blues scale has only six tones
2. Blues scale uses a *1 1/2* step in its step pattern
3. Blues scale has two consecutive half steps in its pattern

CREATING A BLUES SCALE FROM SCRATCH

You have several options when creating a blues scale on a particular root note. Creating blues scales will help you later to create cool solo riffs or licks in any key.

Apply the Step Pattern

One way to create a blues scale is to find the root note and apply the step pattern for each note.

Here is the step pattern for the blues scale. Remember, it incorporates two *1 1/2* steps, as well as two consecutive half steps. (What a weirdo, huh?)

1 1/2–Whole–Half–Half–1 1/2–Whole

Blues Scale Beginning on F:

Create from a Pentatonic Minor Scale

The *pentatonic minor* scale is the simplest tool for making a blues scale. In two easy steps, you'll have a brand new blues scale. Here's how it's done:

1. Create a pentatonic minor scale on the desired root note.

Step pattern = 1 1/2–Whole–Whole–1 1/2

F Pentatonic Minor Scale:

2. Add the note between the fourth and fifth scale degrees.

That's it! You're finished! You have a blues scale now.

Note: You should also commit the minor pentatonic scale to memory, as it comes in handy (pardon the pun, please) when creating blues licks.

Another Blues Scale

Do you know about the concept of the *relative minor?* Every major key has a related minor key, one that shares the same key signature. For example, C major and A minor—no sharps and no flats.

We can extend this idea to scales and use it to get another device to make blues licks. The C blues scale has the notes C E♭ F F♯ G and B♭, but if you've been listening to blues music, you'll notice that there are blues sounds not present in that scale.

By going to the relative minor, A, and building a blues scale there, we can get a whole bunch of other blues sounds. The A blues scale has the notes A C D D♯ E and G. Now we have a whole lotta notes to make blues riffs. Notice which notes are "new," or not present, in the C blues scale: D, E, and A. Most notably, the E is the 3rd of the C, or I, chord and the A is the 3rd of the F, or IV, chord. When you combine these scales or even just use the D♯ moving into E sound, you'll hear a host of typical blues melodic movements and have a much larger palate of sounds.

Blues Scales in Other Keys

To save you going to the bookstore again for a scale book, here is the blues scale in all twelve keys.

C Blues Scale:

D♭ Blues Scale:

D Blues Scale:

E♭ Blues Scale:

E Blues Scale:

F Blues Scale:

F# Blues Scale:

G Blues Scale:

A♭ Blues Scale:

A Blues Scale:

B♭ Blues Scale:

B Blues Scale:

RIFFING IT!

Why is the blues scale so darn important? Because from the blues scale we can create blues riffs. (A *riff* is a short musical idea repeated over and over.)

RIFF BLUES

Many blues songs are created entirely from one little riff, which is repeated again and again over the same 12-bar chord progression. This type of song is called *riff blues*. Here's an example of a riff that could be used in such a blues song:

But imagine playing that same riff twelve times over the 12-bar progression. It would be monotonous and quite boring. So, you change it, but only slightly.

CALL AND RESPONSE

All you need is to give that simple little riff an "answer." That is, another little lick that goes with it and completes it somehow. (Note: A lick is a short musical idea, like a riff, but usually not repeated as a riff would be. Licks are typically used in solos or in improvisations. But you should also know that some folks use the words *riff* and *lick* interchangeably.)

This "answer" is called *call and response*, and is used in virtually every type of musical form, from classical to hip-hop and beyond. The riff will be the call (or question):

Now we simply give it a response (or answer) by creating another idea from the blues scale:

Now you have a call-and-response idea. But when do you play each one? Hey, that's up to you. One of the best things to do, though, is to firmly establish the call before giving away the response. (Make 'em beg for an answer!)

To do this, play the first riff three times (three bars) and answer it in the fourth bar. Over a 12-bar chord progression, you can do this three times:

EXPANDING THE IDEA

To really finesse your blues solo, make a bigger statement with your call-and-response ideas. All you have to do is change the ending.

In a 12-bar blues progression, you can think of the ending as the last four bars. So, play your call-and-response ideas a couple of times (over the first eight bars) and then answer the entire thing with a new 4-bar riff.

NEED SOME IDEAS?

Sure, four bars is a long time and a lot of original notes to come up with. Well, then…cheat! Don't worry about being original. Pick one of these options:

1. Play the blues scale from top to bottom as your ending.

2. Rest for three bars and just make up a 1-bar ending.

3. Play chords over the ending.

If you do it with attitude, your audience won't even notice a lack of originality. Heck, they just want you to get back to the call-and-response part again anyway!

DON'T BE AFRAID TO REST OR REPEAT

Actually, the second option I mentioned on the previous page shouldn't be laughed at. Seriously, don't be afraid to use rests throughout your blues.

A riff can literally be one-note long. That's right! You could play the same note over and over during a 12-bar progression, changing up the rhythm as you go along. Save your really killer riff for the big ending.

Say you come up with this great riff:

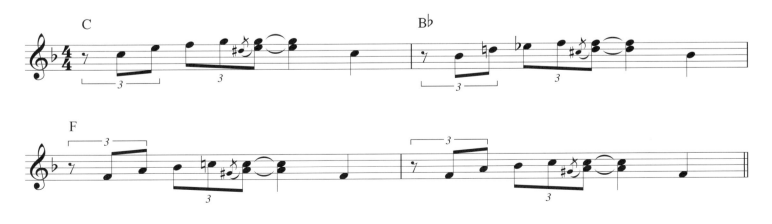

Don't use it! Instead, play a one-note, shifting rhythm solo over eight bars. (Your left hand still plays the chords.)
Then, after you've sufficiently built up the musical tension, knock 'em out with that great riff you've been saving:

Another way to involve rests and build up the tension is the additive approach. What you do is add on to the riff each time it repeats. Starting with one note, notice how the riff expands over the 12-bar progression, and notice the healthy supply of rests at the beginning.

D**R**ESS UP T**H**E NOTES

Even a lame riff can be brought to life with a few effects thrown in. These effects are called *embellishments* or *ornaments*.

GRACE NOTES IN MELODIES

A *grace note* is a note without any real rhythmic value. It's played just slightly before the main note, so that you create a sort of "slide" into that note. Grace notes are notated like this (a little eighth note with a slash through the stem):

You will also encounter multiple grace notes, which are usually notated as little sixteenth notes. These are the same effect: You play them very quickly before the main note. The more grace notes, the more of a slide effect you get:

Try playing a riff without grace notes:

Now add in some amazing grace (notes):

These aren't always easy to play, so practice them often until you can barely even hear the attack of the second note. You want it to sound as if you are "bending" into the note.

GRACE NOTES WITH CHORDS

You can also add grace notes to chords, which is even more difficult but even more effective.

To do this, don't try to play the grace note before the chord. Instead, play the whole chord but with the grace note replacing the note it will slide into. Then immediately make the slide from grace note to "main note" while still holding down the rest of the chord.

As I said, it isn't easy. The most effective note to slide into is the 3rd of the chord. Why? Think about the difference between a major and minor chord. The difference is the type of 3rd used:

Major 3rd   Minor 3rd

By making the grace note one half step lower than the 3rd of the chord, you are momentarily fooling the listener. They think it will be a minor chord (C–E♭–G), but it resolves to a major chord (C–E–G). So tricky are you! (You may wonder why the E♭ is written as a D♯ here. The motion from the grace note to the adjacent "main note" is much clearer visually if the grace note is placed at the adjacent position—line or space—on the staff, not the same position. So the grace note E♭, sliding to E♮, is written as D♯.)

Sounds like a C minor
chord (C-E♭-G) until
the grace note slides.

So, find the 3rd of whichever chord you're playing and add a grace note a half step lower. Practice this effect over a 12-bar progression. Take it slowly the first three or four (hundred) times…

BLUE NOTES

Sure, you could use any note as a grace note, so why is a half step below the 3rd such a big deal?

Let's remember how the blues scale was constructed for a moment. You take a minor pentatonic and insert the note between the fourth and fifth degrees:

Inserted note

That very special note is aptly named the *blue note*.

This note, when inserted into a scale, melody, or riff, sounds "out of the key" and, for some unexplainable psychological reason, bluesy. Without it, you'd just have a minor pentatonic scale or riff. You want proof?

Here's a riff based on the C pentatonic major scale (or if you prefer, the relative minor—the A pentatonic minor scale)…

So here's the same riff with the addition of a blue note…just think of the A pentatonic minor with the addition of a note between the fourth and fifth degrees, a D♯.

TRILLS AND TREMOLOS

Here are two more great effects for blues solos. With both trills and tremolos, you are rapidly alternating between a main note and another note. The main difference is the size of the interval between the notes.

A trill involves two notes that are a half or whole step apart. It's notated with a "tr" above the note, which means to rapidly alternate between the written note and the next scale step above. In the example below, in the key of C, the alternation is between F and G.

If you see a *tr* plus a flat sign, this means to trill upward to the note a half step lower than the next scale step above. In the example below, in the key of C, the alternation is between G and A♭.

A tremolo is like a trill, but it involves notes that are more than a whole step apart (either upward or downward). It's generally notated with three beams between the notes, with both the main note and secondary (alternating) note receiving the full rhythmic value of the main note. In the example below, alternate rapidly between the notes, G and B, for the duration of a half note.

Try playing some trills and tremolos in a solo riff blues:

TREMOLO CHORDS AND CLUSTERS

As if tremolos and trills between two notes wasn't fun enough, you also get to tremolo chords. All you do is divide the chord into two parts and rock your hand between these two parts quickly, so that it sounds like the chord is "shaking."

Another way to break up a chord is to play the notes of the chord individually like a very, very fast arpeggio:

Sometimes you'll encounter a cluster of notes that don't really make a chord. Playing these as tremolos also sounds very bluesy:

LOTS OF RIFFS

With the many rhythms, tricks, effects, embellishments, and scales you've learned so far, you're ready to start making your own blues riffs.

But in times of noncreativity, when your brain is frozen, you can turn to these pages for some ideas and inspiration. Play them as they are, combine them, transpose them to other keys. However you choose to use them, you'll be playing the blues…

RIGHT-HAND RIFFS

Use these for solos over a cool chord progression.

LEFT-HAND RIFFS

Use these under right-hand chords or solos. (Of course, the latter is quite tricky and will take more practice.)

INTROS

Every great song has to have a cool intro.

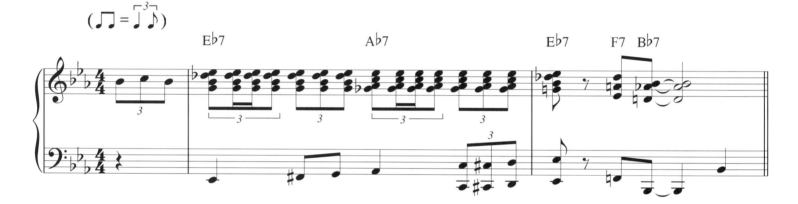

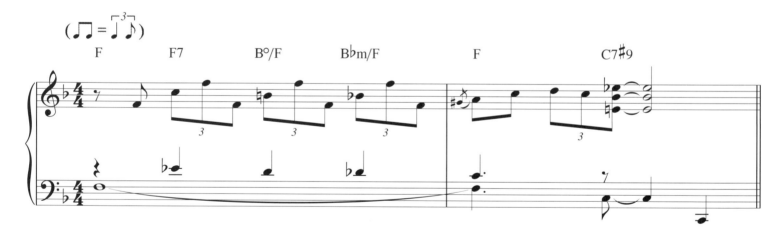

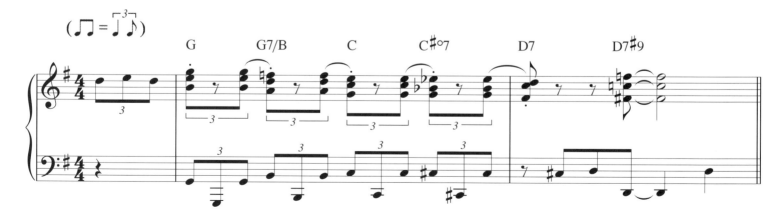

OUTROS

And every great song has to have a show-stopping outro.

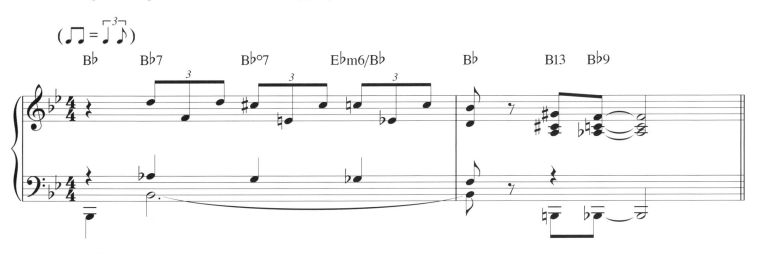

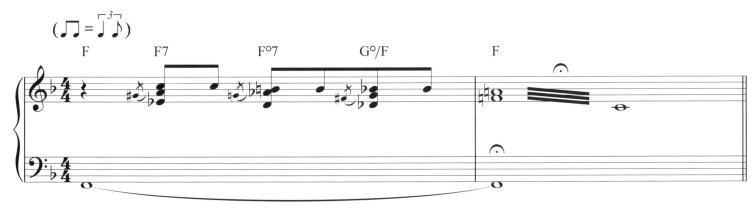

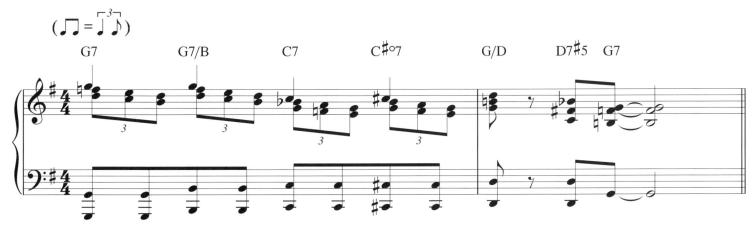

Thanks for playing. See ya next time!

More Big-Note & Easy Piano Books

For a complete listing of Cherry Lane titles available, including contents listings, please visit our web site at www.cherrylane.

CHOPIN FOR EASY PIANO
This special easy piano version features the composer's intricate melodies, harmonies and rhythms newly arranged so that virtually all pianists can experience the thrill of playing Chopin at the piano! Includes 20 favorites mazurkas, nocturnes, polonaises, preludes and waltzes.
_____02501483 Easy Piano...............$7.99

CLASSICAL CHRISTMAS
Easy solo arrangements of 30 wonderful holiday songs: Ave Maria • Dance of the Sugar Plum Fairy • Evening Prayer • Gesu Bambino • Hallelujah! • He Shall Feed His Flock • March of the Toys • O Come, All Ye Faithful • O Holy Night • Pastoral Symphony • Sheep May Safely Graze • Sinfonia • Waltz of the Flowers • and more.
_____02500112 Easy Piano Solo.......$9.95

BEST OF JOHN DENVER
A collection of 18 Denver classics, including: Leaving on a Jet Plane • Take Me Home, Country Roads • Rocky Mountain High • Follow Me • and more.
_____02505512 Easy Piano...............$9.95

JOHN DENVER ANTHOLOGY
Easy arrangements of 34 of the finest from this beloved artist. Includes: Annie's Song • Fly Away • Follow Me • Grandma's Feather Bed • Leaving on a Jet Plane • Perhaps Love • Rocky Mountain High • Sunshine on My Shoulders • Take Me Home, Country Roads • Thank God I'm a Country Boy • and many more.
_____02501366 Easy Piano.............$19.99

EASY BROADWAY SHOWSTOPPERS
Easy piano arrangements of 16 traditional and new Broadway standards, including: "Impossible Dream" from *Man of La Mancha* • "Unusual Way" from *Nine* • "This Is the Moment" from *Jekyll & Hyde* • many more.
_____02505517 Easy Piano.............$12.95

A FAMILY CHRISTMAS AROUND THE PIANO
25 songs for hours of family fun, including: Away in a Manger • Deck the Hall • The First Noel • God Rest Ye Merry, Gentlemen • Hark! the Herald Angels Sing • Jingle Bells • Jolly Old St. Nicholas • Joy to the World • O Little Town of Bethlehem • Silent Night, Holy Night • The Twelve Days of Christmas • and more.
_____02500398 Easy Piano...............$8.99

FAVORITE CELTIC SONGS FOR EASY PIANO
Easy arrangements of 40 Celtic classics, including: The Ash Grove • The Bluebells of Scotland • A Bunch of Thyme • Danny Boy • Finnegan's Wake • I'll Tell Me Ma • Loch Lomond • My Wild Irish Rose • The Rose of Tralee • and more!
_____02501306 Easy Piano.............$12.99

FAVORITE POP BALLADS
This new collection features 35 beloved ballads, including: Breathe (2 AM) • Faithfully • Leaving on a Jet Plane • Open Arms • Ordinary People • Summer Breeze • These Eyes • Truly • You've Got a Friend • and more.
_____02501005 Easy Piano............$15.99

HOLY CHRISTMAS CAROLS COLORING BOOK
A terrific songbook with 7 sacred carols and lots of coloring pages for the young pianist. Songs include: Angels We Have Heard on High • The First Noel • Hark! The Herald Angels Sing • It Came upon a Midnight Clear • O Come All Ye Faithful • O Little Town of Bethlehem • Silent Night.
_____02500277 Five-Finger Piano $6.95

JEKYLL & HYDE — VOCAL SELECTIONS
Ten songs from the Wildhorn/Bricusse Broadway smash, arranged for big-note: In His Eyes • It's a Dangerous Game • Lost in the Darkness • A New Life • No One Knows Who I Am • Once Upon a Dream • Someone Like You • Sympathy, Tenderness • Take Me as I Am • This Is the Moment.
_____02500023 Big-Note Piano $9.95

JACK JOHNSON ANTHOLOGY
Easy arrangements of 27 of the best from this Hawaiian singer/songwriter, including: Better Together • Breakdown • Flake • Fortunate Fool • Good People • Sitting, Waiting, Wishing • Taylor • and more.
_____02501313 Easy Piano............$19.99

JUST FOR KIDS – NOT! CHRISTMAS SONGS
This unique collection of 14 Christmas favorites is fun for the whole family! Kids can play the full-sounding big-note solos alone, or with their parents (or teachers) playing accompaniment for the thrill of four-hand piano! Includes: Deck the Halls • Jingle Bells • Silent Night • What Child Is This? • and more.
_____02505510 Big-Note Piano $8.95

JUST FOR KIDS – NOT! CLASSICS
Features big-note arrangements of classical masterpieces, plus optional accompaniment for adults. Songs: Air on the G String • Dance of the Sugar Plum Fairy • Für Elise • Jesu, Joy of Man's Desiring • Ode to Joy • Pomp and Circumstance • The Sorcerer's Apprentice • William Tell Overture • and more!
_____02505513 Classics $7.95
_____02500301 More Classics..........$8.95

JUST FOR KIDS – NOT! FUN SONGS
Fun favorites for kids everywhere in big-note arrangements for piano, including: Bingo • Eensy Weensy Spider • Farmer in the Dell • Jingle Bells • London Bridge • Pop Goes the Weasel • Puff the Magic Dragon • Skip to My Lou • Twinkle, Twinkle Little Star • and more!
_____02505523 Fun Songs $7.95

JUST FOR KIDS – NOT! TV THEMES & MOVIE SONGS
Entice the kids to the piano with this delightful collection of songs and themes from movies and TV. These big-note arrangements include themes from The Brady Bunch and The Addams Family, as well as Do-Re-Mi (The Sound of Music), theme from Beetlejuice (Day-O) and Puff the Magic Dragon. Each song includes an accompaniment part for teacher or adult so that the kids can experience the joy of four-hand playing as well! Plus performance tips.
_____02505507 TV Themes & Movie Songs.....................$9.95
_____02500304 More TV Themes & Movie Songs.....................$9.95

MERRY CHRISTMAS, EVERYONE
Over 20 contemporary and classic all-time holiday favorites arranged for big-note piano or easy piano. Includes: Away in a Manger • Christmas Like a Lullaby • The First Noel • Joy to the World • The Marvelous Toy • and more.
_____02505600 Big-Note Piano $9.95

POKEMON 2 B.A. MASTER
This great songbook features easy piano arrangements of 13 tunes from the hit TV series: 2.B.A. Master • Double Trouble (Team Rocket) • Everything Changes • Misty's Song • My Best Friends • Pokémon (Dance Mix) • Pokémon Theme • PokéRAP • The Time Has Come (Pikachu's Goodbye) • Together, Forever • Viridian City • What Kind of Pokémon Are You? • You Can Do It (If You Really Try). Includes a full-color, 8-page pull-out section featuring characters and scenes from this super hot show.
_____02500145 Easy Piano.............$12.95

POP/ROCK LOVE SONGS
Easy arrangements of 18 romatic favorites, including: Always • Bed of Roses • Butterfly Kisses • Follow Me • From This Moment On • Hard Habit to Break • Leaving on a Jet Plane • When You Say Nothing at All • more.
_____02500151 Easy Piano.............$10.95

POPULAR CHRISTMAS CAROLS COLORING BOOK
Kids are sure to love this fun holiday songbook! It features five-finger piano arrangements of seven Christmas classics, complete with coloring pages throughout! Songs include: Deck the Hall • Good King Wenceslas • Jingle Bells • Jolly Old St. Nicholas • O Christmas Tree • Up on the Housetop • We Wish You a Merry Christmas.
_____02500276 Five-Finger Piano $6.95

PUFF THE MAGIC DRAGON & 54 OTHER ALL-TIME CHILDREN'S FAVORITESONGS
55 timeless songs enjoyed by generations of kids, and sure to be favorites for years to come. Songs include: A-Tisket A-Tasket • Alouette • Eensy Weensy Spider • The Farmer in the Dell • I've Been Working on the Railroad • If You're Happy and You Know It • Joy to the World • Michael Finnegan • Oh Where, Oh Where Has My Little Dog Gone • Silent Night • Skip to My Lou • This Old Man • and many more.
_____02500017 Big-Note Piano $12.95

See your local music dealer or contact:

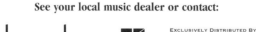

cherry lane
music company

EXCLUSIVELY DISTRIBUTED BY
HAL•LEONARD®
7777 W. BLUEMOUND RD. P.O. BOX 13819 MILWAUKEE, WI 53213

Prices, contents, and availability subject to change without notice.

0811

great songs series

This legendary series has delighted players and performers for generations.

Great Songs of the Fifties

Features rock, pop, country, Broadway and movie tunes, including: All Shook Up • At the Hop • Blue Suede Shoes • Dream Lover • Fly Me to the Moon • Kansas City • Love Me Tender • Misty • Peggy Sue • Rock Around the Clock • Sea of Love • Sixteen Tons • Take the "A" Train • Wonderful! Wonderful! • and more. Includes an introduction by award-winning journalist Bruce Pollock.
02500323 P/V/G.....................................$16.95

Great Songs of the Sixties, Vol. 1 – Revised

The updated version of this classic book includes 80 faves from the 1960s: Angel of the Morning • Bridge over Troubled Water • Cabaret • Different Drum • Do You Believe in Magic • Eve of Destruction • Monday, Monday • Spinning Wheel • Walk on By • and more.
02509902 P/V/G.....................................$19.95

Great Songs of the Sixties, Vol. 2 – Revised

61 more '60s hits: California Dreamin' • Crying • For Once in My Life • Honey • Little Green Apples • MacArthur Park • Me and Bobby McGee • Nowhere Man • Piece of My Heart • Sugar, Sugar • You Made Me So Very Happy • and more.
02509904 P/V/G.....................................$19.95

Great Songs of the Seventies, Vol. 1 – Revised

This super collection of 70 big hits from the '70s includes: After the Love Has Gone • Afternoon Delight • Annie's Song • Band on the Run • Cold as Ice • FM • Imagine • It's Too Late • Layla • Let It Be • Maggie May • Piano Man • Shelter from the Storm • Superstar • Sweet Baby James • Time in a Bottle • The Way We Were • and more.
02509917 P/V/G.....................................$19.95

Great Songs of the Eighties – Revised

This edition features 50 songs in rock, pop & country styles, plus hits from Broadway and the movies! Songs: Almost Paradise • Angel of the Morning • Do You Really Want to Hurt Me • Endless Love • Flashdance...What a Feeling • Guilty • Hungry Eyes • (Just Like) Starting Over • Let Love Rule • Missing You • Patience • Through the Years • Time After Time • Total Eclipse of the Heart • and more.
02502125 P/V/G.....................................$18.95

Great Songs of the Nineties

Includes: Achy Breaky Heart • Beautiful in My Eyes • Believe • Black Hole Sun • Black Velvet • Blaze of Glory • Building a Mystery • Crash into Me • Fields of Gold • From a Distance • Glycerine • Here and Now • Hold My Hand • I'll Make Love to You • Ironic • Linger • My Heart Will Go On • Waterfalls • Wonderwall • and more.
02500040 P/V/G.....................................$16.95

Great Songs of 2000-2009

Over 50 of the decade's biggest hits, including: Accidentally in Love • Breathe (2 AM) • Daughters • Hanging by a Moment • The Middle • The Remedy (I Won't Worry) • Smooth • A Thousand Miles • and more.
02500922 P/V/G.....................................$24.99

Great Songs of Broadway – Revised Edition

This updated edition is loaded with 54 hits: And All That Jazz • Be Italian • Comedy Tonight • Consider Yourself • Dulcinea • Edelweiss • Friendship • Getting to Know You • Hopelessly Devoted to You • If I Loved You • The Impossible Dream • Mame • On My Own • On the Street Where You Live • People • Try to Remember • Unusual Way • When You're Good to Mama • Where Is Love? • and more.
02501545 P/V/G.....................................$19.99

Great Songs for Children

90 wonderful, singable favorites kids love: Baa Baa Black Sheep • Bingo • The Candy Man • Do-Re-Mi • Eensy Weensy Spider • The Hokey Pokey • Linus and Lucy • Sing • This Old Man • Yellow Submarine • and more, with a touching foreword by Grammy-winning singer/songwriter Tom Chapin.
02501348 P/V/G.....................................$19.99

Prices, contents, and availability subject to change without notice.

Great Songs of Christmas

59 yuletide favorites in piano/vocal/guitar format, including: Breath of Heaven (Mary's Song) • Christmas Time Is Here • Frosty the Snow Man • I'll Be Home for Christmas • Jingle-Bell Rock • Nuttin' for Christmas • O Little Town of Bethlehem • Silver Bells • The Twelve Days of Christmas • What Child Is This? • and many more.
02501543 P/V/G.....................................$17.99

Great Songs of Country Music

This volume features 58 country gems, including: Abilene • Afternoon Delight • Amazed • Annie's Song • Blue • Crazy • Elvira • Fly Away • For the Good Times • Friends in Low Places • The Gambler • Hey, Good Lookin' • I Hope You Dance • Thank God I'm a Country Boy • This Kiss • Your Cheatin' Heart • and more.
02500503 P/V/G.....................................$19.95

Great Songs of Folk Music

Nearly 50 of the most popular folk songs of our time, including: Blowin' in the Wind • The House of the Rising Sun • Puff the Magic Dragon • This Land Is Your Land • Time in a Bottle • The Times They Are A-Changin' • The Unicorn • Where Have All the Flowers Gone? • and more.
02500997 P/V/G.....................................$19.95

Great Songs from The Great American Songbook

52 American classics, including: Ain't That a Kick in the Head • As Time Goes By • Come Fly with Me • Georgia on My Mind • I Get a Kick Out of You • I've Got You Under My Skin • The Lady Is a Tramp • Love and Marriage • Mack the Knife • Misty • Over the Rainbow • People • Take the "A" Train • Thanks for the Memory • and more.
02500760 P/V/G.....................................$16.95

Great Songs of the Movies

Nearly 60 of the best songs popularized in the movies, including: Accidentally in Love • Alfie • Almost Paradise • The Rainbow Connection • Somewhere in My Memory • Take My Breath Away (Love Theme) • Three Coins in the Fountain • (I've Had) the Time of My Life • Up Where We Belong • The Way We Were • and more.
02500967 P/V/G.....................................$19.95

Great Songs of the Pop Era

Over 50 hits from the pop era, including: Every Breath You Take • I'm Every Woman • Just the Two of Us • Leaving on a Jet Plane • My Cherie Amour • Raindrops Keep Fallin' on My Head • Time After Time • (I've Had) the Time of My Life • What a Wonderful World • and more.
02500043 Easy Piano.............................$16.95

Great Songs for Weddings

A beautiful collection of 59 pop standards perfect for wedding ceremonies and receptions, including: Always and Forever • Amazed • Beautiful in My Eyes • Can You Feel the Love Tonight • Endless Love • Love of a Lifetime • Open Arms • Unforgettable • When I Fall in Love • The Wind Beneath My Wings • and more.
02501006 P/V/G.....................................$19.95

 cherry lane music company
www.cherrylane.com

 EXCLUSIVELY DISTRIBUTED BY HAL•LEONARD CORPORATION
7777 W. BLUEMOUND RD. P.O. BOX 13819 MILWAUKEE, WI 53213

0411

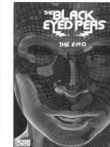

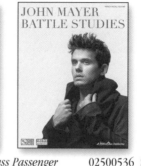